Visual Geography Series®

ALBANIA

...in Pictures

Prepared by
Geography Department

Lerner Publications Company
Minneapolis

Copyright © 1995 by Lerner Publications Company

Photo © Massimo Sciacca

A boy carries a heavy sack of food that a foreign country has donated to Albania. Shortages of food and other goods affect many Albanian cities and towns.

This book is a newly commissioned title in the Visual Geography Series. The text is set in 10/12 Century Textbook.

LIBRARY OF CONGRESS CATALOGING-IN-PUBLICATION DATA

Albania in pictures / prepared by Geography Department, Lerner Publications Company.

p. cm. — (Visual geography series)
Includes index.
ISBN 0-8225-1902-X (lib. bdg.)
1. Albania. [1. Albania.]   I. Lerner Publications Company. Geography Dept. II. Series: Visual geography series (Minneapolis, Minn.)
DR943.A4   1995   94-10616
949.65 – dc20   CIP
                                                      AC

International Standard Book Number: 0-8225-1902-X
Library of Congress Catalog Card Number: 94-10616

VISUAL GEOGRAPHY SERIES®

Publisher
Harry Jonas Lerner
Senior Editor
Mary M. Rodgers
Editors
Tom Streissguth
Colleen Sexton
Photo Researcher
Erica Ackerberg
Editorial/Photo Assistant
Marybeth Campbell
Consultants/Contributors
Isuf Hajrizi
Frank Jossi
Sandra K. Davis
Designer
Jim Simondet
Cartographer
Carol F. Barrett
Indexer
Sylvia Timian
Production Manager
Gary J. Hansen

Courtesy of Illyria, The Albanian-American Newspaper, NY

Traditional homes line a quiet, cobblestoned street in the southern city of Korce.

Acknowledgments

Title page photo by Frank Jossi.

Elevation contours adapted from *The Times Atlas of the World*, seventh comprehensive edition (New York: Times Books, 1985).

Albanian accents, which affect Albanian pronunciation, have not been used in this book.

1 2 3 4 5 6 – I/JR – 00 99 98 97 96 95

The ruins of an ancient castle loom over the hills near Kruje. In the mid-fifteenth century, this stronghold was the headquarters of Skanderbeg, the national hero of Albania.

Contents

MONTENEGRO

SERBIA

KOSOVO

BULGARIA

L. Shkoder   *Drin R.*

Shkoder

Buna R.

ADRIATIC

SEA

Lezhe

Mat R.

Drini i Zi

Kruje

Bulquiza R.

MACEDONIA

⊕ TIRANE

Durres
EPIDAMNOS
(Ruins)

Elbasan

Shkumbin R.

Lake Oher

Lushnje

Lake Prespa

Pogradec

APOLLONIA
(Ruins)

Berat

Little Lake Prespa

Bay of Vlore

Vjose R.

Korce

GREECE

Strait of Otranto

Vlore

Tepelene

N
↑

ALBANIA

- - - Administrative Boundaries

——— Major Roads

Gjirokaster

Drino R.

| 0 | | 25 | | 50 | Miles |
| 0 | 25 | | 50 | Kilometers | |

ITALY

Sarande

Butrint

Ioannina

CORFU I.

EPIRUS

EUROPE
ALBANIA

Arctic Circle

NORWEGIAN
SEA

20°   0°   20°

80°   60°

NORTH
ATLANTIC
OCEAN

20°

40°

MEDITERRANEAN SEA

40°

0°   20°

| 0 | 400 Miles | |
| 0 | 400 Kilometers | |

METRIC CONVERSION CHART
To Find Approximate Equivalents

WHEN YOU KNOW:	MULTIPLY BY:	TO FIND:
AREA		
acres	0.41	hectares
square miles	2.59	square kilometers
CAPACITY		
gallons	3.79	liters
LENGTH		
feet	30.48	centimeters
yards	0.91	meters
miles	1.61	kilometers
MASS (weight)		
pounds	0.45	kilograms
tons	0.91	metric tons
VOLUME		
cubic yards	0.77	cubic meters
TEMPERATURE		
degrees Fahrenheit	0.56 (*after* subtracting 32)	degrees Celsius

Photo © Massimo Sciacca

Patrons of a bakery in the Albanian capital of Tirane wait for their bread. Like many Albanian businesses, this shop was privatized—sold to private owners—by the government after Communist rule ended in 1992.

Introduction

Albania, a small and mountainous nation in southern Europe, has a long and turbulent history. For centuries the country suffered conquest and foreign occupation. In more recent years, Albanian leaders cut off trade and communication with other nations. Although these policies caused terrible economic problems, they also helped the Albanians to preserve a unique culture with ancient roots.

Ethnic Albanians claim descent from the Illyrians, a people that invaded southern Europe's Balkan Peninsula more than 3,000 years ago. Later the ancient Greeks

built ports and towns in the area, and the Roman Empire established a province of Illyricum in the Balkans. But many Illyrians remained fiercely independent, and the collapse of the Roman Empire in the fifth century A.D. left the Balkan region in turmoil.

For the next 1,000 years, the Albanians—who were named after an Illyrian group—lived without a central government. Feuding dynasties (ruling families) and powerful landowners controlled small territories in Albania's river valleys and rugged highlands. Foreign governments,

Children in Tirane give the victory sign as a new democratic government takes power.

such as the Italian republic of Venice, built ports and trading posts in Albania's coastal lowlands.

In the fifteenth century, the Ottoman Turks invaded the Balkan Peninsula from their base in Asia Minor (modern Turkey). The Ottomans ruled the area by making vassals (servants) of the Albanian landowners. Under Turkish rule, trade declined in the cities and ports of the region. With limited fertile land available for farming, Albania could produce little. The country's main exports were weapons and mercenary soldiers.

In 1912 Albania declared its independence from the Ottoman Empire. But after a group of European politicians drew new borders for the nation, millions of Albanians were stranded in neighboring coun-

Women weave elaborate carpets by hand at a rug factory in Tirane. Before World War II (1939–1945), small factories and workshops dominated Albania's industrial sector.

Vendors offer auto parts for sale to passersby. To support themselves, many Albanians take part in an "underground" economy, in which they sell goods outside of government control and taxation.

tries. During World War I (1914–1918) and World War II (1939–1945), Albania became a battleground for foreign powers seeking control of the Balkan Peninsula.

After World War II ended, Albanian Communists took power under Enver Hoxha, a wartime guerrilla leader. Fearful of foreign invasion and determined to build a pure Communist state, Hoxha eventually cut Albania's ties to all of its Communist allies, including Yugoslavia, the Soviet Union, and China. The Albanian Communist party—the nation's only legal political organization—ruthlessly stamped out opposition at home.

By the early 1980s, Albania had neither economic partners nor political allies. Hoxha's policies had stopped all foreign investment, and the nation's manufacturing sector declined. As production fell, shortages of food and factory goods be-

came common. By the time of Hoxha's death in 1985, Albania was the poorest nation in Europe.

With the fall of the Communist regime in the early 1990s, a new era in Albania's history began. In 1992 a democratic government promised to reform the nation's economy. Foreign countries are again investing in Albania, which has gained important trading partners. For the first time in many years, visitors are welcome, and Albania is even trying to develop a tourism industry.

Yet Albanians still suffer poverty, shortages of food and consumer goods, and a lack of economic opportunity. Ethnic conflicts in neighboring Balkan nations also threaten to drag the country into another war. Despite the many changes in its government and economy, Albania faces a long struggle to reach stability and prosperity.

Olive trees surround a house in the Albanian countryside. The trees thrive in Albania's dry climate and provide a fruit that can be eaten or pressed into cooking oil.

1) The Land

The Republic of Albania lies on the Balkan Peninsula in southern Europe. To the north and northeast are Montenegro and Serbia, respectively. These two republics make up the remaining territory of Yugoslavia, a nation that broke up in the early 1990s. Albania's eastern neighbor is Macedonia, and to the southeast lies Greece. The Adriatic Sea, an arm of the Mediterranean Sea, forms a long western coastline and separates Albania from Italy.

Covering 11,100 square miles, Albania is about the same size as the state of Maryland. Mountains dominate the Albanian landscape, but most of the country's people live in a narrow coastal lowland in the west. Small towns and villages have been built in the river valleys of the east and south, while isolated settlements dot northern Albania's rugged highlands. The greatest distance from north to south is 211 miles. From east to west, Albania stretches 93 miles at its widest point.

Topography

Albania's isolation from the rest of Europe results partly from its mountainous landscape. Steep ranges cut the nation off from its Balkan neighbors. Westward-flowing rivers rush through the gorges and narrow valleys of these mountains, which give way to a flat and sandy lowland in the west. Roads in the Albanian highlands are poor, and motor vehicles still cannot reach much of the country.

The North Albanian Alps extend 20 miles southward from Albania's border with Montenegro. Ancient glaciers (ice masses) carved the deep ravines of this range, where snow covers the highest ridges throughout the year. Isolated pastures provide some grazing land for livestock, but most of the region is too steep and rocky for growing crops. Southwest of these mountains are the grassy slopes and rounded peaks of the Cukali Highlands, which overlook the valley of the Drin River.

The Central Highlands of Albania are a series of small ranges that run 70 miles from the Drin southward to the Shkumbin River. Elevations here average about 2,000 feet above sea level, with some peaks reaching 5,000 feet. Mount Korab, Albania's highest point, rises 9,026 feet on the border with Macedonia. A few narrow and

Before the twentieth century, Albania had few bridges, and travelers crossed wide or fast rivers with rafts or ferries. After World War II (1939–1945), the Communist regime built many new roads and bridges, such as this one in southern Albania.

Mountains rise above the Bulquiza River of central Albania. Many rivers in Albania's highlands run between steep cliffs, forcing cars and pedestrians to use narrow tracks.

twisting roads link the Central Highlands to the lowlands in the west. River valleys and small basins (level plains surrounded by higher elevations) have attracted most of the area's settlers.

Small plateaus lie among the hills and mountains of the Southern Highlands, which extend into northern Greece. Vineyards and fruit orchards crowd the Korce Basin, an important agricultural region in the southeast. The steep Nemercke and Grammos ranges tower over the Vijose River Valley, which serves as an important transportation route between Albania and Greece. South of the port of Vlore, the Southern Highlands rise above a narrow strip of bays and inlets along the seacoast. In the far south, across a narrow strait, lies the Greek island of Corfu.

Albania's Coastal Lowlands stretch from Lake Shkoder in the north to Vlore in the south, a distance of about 120 miles. Irrigation channels in the lowlands support extensive farming. Beaches and lagoons line the Adriatic coast, where silt from upland valleys forms muddy deltas at the mouths of Albania's rivers. The Myzeqeja Plain, an area of swamps and irrigated farmland, extends 30 miles inland from the sea to the city of Elbasan.

Courtesy of Illyria, The Albanian-American Newspaper, NY

The waters of the Adriatic Sea break against rocky cliffs in southern Albania. Many dramatic capes have been formed where the mountain ranges of the area meet the sea.

Courtesy of Illyria, The Albanian-American Newspaper, NY

A small village nestles among the hills and vegetation that are common in central Albania. Small, hardy trees and a shrub known as maquis thrive in the dry, rocky soil of the region.

Albania's Communist regime ordered the construction of thousands of concrete bunkers to defend against attack by hostile nations. The bunkers still dot the landscape near cities, towns, and rivers, making farming and new construction difficult.

Rivers and Lakes

As Albania's rivers travel westward toward the Adriatic Sea, they carry gravel, silt, and rich clay soil down from the highlands. But much of this sediment flows into marshes that line the rivers in the Coastal Lowlands. As a result, for most of Albania's history this area could support very little farming.

In the early 1900s, the Albanian government drained hundreds of swamps along the coast to create farmland. Farmers in the lowlands now use the rivers to irrigate fields of grain and vegetable crops. In the mountains, Albania has built hydroelectric power plants on the Drin and on other fast-moving rivers.

The 175-mile-long Drin River rises in eastern Albania, where it is fed by the Drini i Zi River, a long and winding tributary. The Drin crashes through several narrow gorges along its course east and south of the Cukali Highlands. After passing through a swampy lowland, the Drin branches into several channels and empties into the Adriatic Sea near the town of Lezhe.

The Shkumbin and Mat rivers are the principal waterways of central Albania. These rivers often run dry in the summer but become torrents during winter, when precipitation in the mountains is heaviest. The channels of these waterways sometimes change course, creating flat and marshy plains where the rivers once flowed.

The Vijose River runs northwest over the Greek border, passes a series of narrow gorges, and forms the southern edge of the Myzeqeja Plain. In the south, the Drino River, a tributary of the Vijose, travels through a wide valley and past the town of Gjirokaster on its way to the Adriatic Sea.

Three large freshwater lakes lie along the borders of eastern Albania. The clear waters of spring-fed Lake Oher, which Albania shares with Macedonia, are transparent to a depth of 70 feet. The borders of Macedonia, Albania, and Greece meet in the middle of Lake Prespa. Although it lies mainly within Greece, a small portion of Little Lake Prespa stretches into Albania.

11

A man drives a horse-drawn cart past a chemical factory in Tirane.

Several rivers and streams that flow through the North Albanian Alps drain into Lake Shkoder, which straddles Albania's border with Montenegro. The Buna River, the only river in Albania deep enough for commercial ship traffic, links Lake Shkoder to the Adriatic Sea.

Climate

Warm breezes from the Mediterranean Sea, as well as the colder winds of the Balkan Peninsula, affect Albania's changeable climate. Temperatures and rainfall vary greatly from the Coastal Lowlands to the mountainous interior. In recent years, several droughts have struck the country, causing crops to fail and rivers to run dry.

Durres, Vlore, and other cities along the Albanian coast have hot summers, cool winters, and low rainfall. Summer temperatures can top 100° F, although the av-

A road winds through terraced fields near Pogradec, a village on the southern shore of Lake Oher. The snowcapped mountains in the background cross the border between Albania and Macedonia.

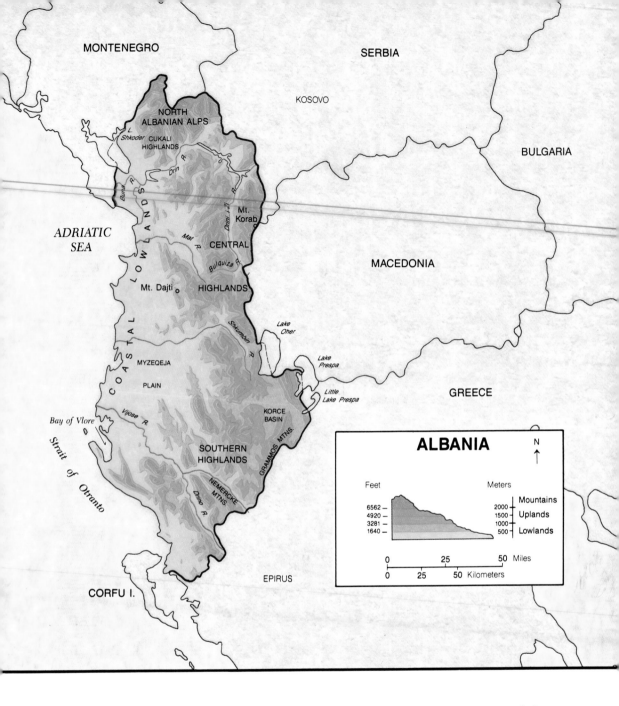

erage temperature in July, the hottest month, is 75° F. Winter brings sudden, heavy thunderstorms to the coast. The sharp *bora* winds, which blow from the north, lower temperatures to an average of 44° F in January, the coldest month.

The country's high mountains protect the coast from severe winter weather, but Albanians who live in highland areas ex-perience cold temperatures and heavy rains between September and May. The average annual precipitation exceeds 100 inches in the North Albanian Alps, where snow covers the highest peaks for much of the year. Farther south, however, tem-peratures are warmer, and precipitation is lighter. During the summer months, nights in the mountains are cool.

Flora and Fauna

Albania's plains and mountains support a wide variety of flora and fauna, but timber cutters and natural fires have transformed many wooded areas into grassland. The loss of trees, which held soil in place with their root systems, has caused deep erosion of many hillsides. Yet forests still cover more than 40 percent of the land, and Albania has begun a reforestation program to repair eroded areas.

Above an elevation of 3,000 feet, stands of oak, beech, birch, elm, and other deciduous (leaf-shedding) trees give way to scattered black pines and other coniferous (evergreen) species. Shrubby plants such as oleander, pomegranate, and chaste trees also thrive at higher elevations. Maquis, a drought-resistant evergreen plant, is common in dry coastal areas.

Deforestation has harmed Albania's wild animals by destroying their natural habitats and food sources. But hares, foxes, deer, and wolves have survived in remote highland areas, and wild goats roam the mountainsides. Ducks, swans, herons, and pelicans live in coastal marshes. In addition to partridges and pheasants, mountain eagles still fly in Albania, whose people call their land *Shqiperi*, meaning "the country of the eagles."

Natural Resources

During their history, Albanians have not had the means to make use of their country's natural resources. With investment from other nations, however, the mining industry quickly developed in the years after World War II. Workers in the north extract valuable chromium ore, a major export, at mines near the Drin and Drini i Zi rivers. Deposits of copper, iron ore, nickel, coal, bitumen (a material used in road construction) and limestone also exist in the highlands of the north and east.

Logging trucks rumble along the dirt roads of northern Albania. Built in the years after World War II, the roads have allowed more extensive timbercutting in this mountainous region, which is the most isolated part of the country.

In the valley of the Bulquiza River, workers stand beside an empty train that a mine uses to transport coal.

Photo © Massimo Sciacca

Albania's energy industry depends on the country's natural resources. Lignite, a soft brown coal, provides fuel for some electricity plants. The rushing waters of the Drin and Mat rivers power hydroelectric plants, which generate surplus energy that Albania can export to neighboring countries.

Albania also claims ownership of several offshore oil fields in the Adriatic Sea. The government has signed agreements with foreign companies that will help extract this valuable fuel source. In the future, Albania may also be able to tap underground reserves of natural gas and asphalt, an important construction material.

Cities

Albania is a rural and largely agricultural country of 3.3 million people. Although the building of new factories after World War II attracted some people into urban centers, the percentage of Albanians who are

Courtesy of Illyria, The Albanian-American Newspaper, NY

A statue of Skanderbeg stands next to a mosque—an Islamic house of prayer—in the central square of Tirane. Skanderbeg fought against the Islamic Turks but died during his campaigns. His successors were unable to stop the occupation of the country, which led to the conversion of most Albanians to Islam.

15

Courtesy of Illyria, The Albanian-American Newspaper, NY

The town of Shkoder lies in a plain between the Adriatic seacoast and the mountains of northern Albania. This view is from the Fortress of Rozafa, an ancient stronghold on the town's outskirts.

city dwellers has reached only 36 percent, a low figure for a European nation. The Coastal Lowlands and the basins of the interior hold the majority of Albanian cities, while the northern and eastern regions have mostly small towns and villages.

TIRANE

Tirane (also spelled Tirana), the nation's capital, lies 50 miles from the Adriatic coast in north central Albania. The slopes of Mount Dajti and other mountains rise near the city, which has a population of 260,000. Main highways lead north, south, and east from Tirane, which links the Coastal Lowlands to the Central Highlands.

The Turkish general Suleyman Pasha Mulleti founded Tirane in 1614. The Turks, who controlled the Balkan Peninsula at that time, built public baths, shops, and a mosque (an Islamic house of prayer) in the city, which remained a quiet outpost of the Ottoman Empire until the early 1900s. In 1920 Albanian officials moved

the national capital to Tirane from Durres, a coastal city that was vulnerable to invasion. After World War II, Tirane grew rapidly as the Communist regime industrialized the country. Factories in the capital, which has become Albania's major manufacturing center, now make foodstuffs, textiles, and heavy machinery.

Tirane also boasts a national art gallery, Albania's oldest and largest university, and a large public park. Government offices and ministries line the six-lane Avenue of Martyrs, the city's main street. The 14-story Hotel Tirane, the tallest building in Albania, faces Skanderbeg Square. This popular plaza was named after a hero of Albania's historic struggle against Ottoman rule.

SECONDARY CITIES

Durres (population 85,000) is Albania's second largest city and the country's leading port. Founded by the Greeks in the seventh century B.C., Durres later became

16

the western endpoint of the Via Egnatia, an important road that linked the Adriatic Sea to the distant city of Constantinople (modern Istanbul, Turkey). In Durres the ancient Romans raised an amphitheater that could seat 20,000 spectators—the largest such structure in the Balkans. After Albania's independence, Durres served as the national capital from 1914 until 1920.

Modern Durres is an important commercial harbor that links Albania to ports in Italy, Greece, and Montenegro. The city is also a center of Albania's small railway system. Factories in Durres produce televisions, radios, cigarettes, tractors, and wine.

Shkoder (population 82,000) is the largest city in northern Albania. The Illyrians made Shkoder the capital of their ancient empire nearly 2,500 years ago. The imposing Fortress of Rozafa, which overlooks

Photo © Massimo Sciacca

Two friends pose in a vacant lot in Durres, Albania's most important port and second largest city.

Photo by Diane Katsiaficas

Albania's 3.3 million people are divided among two main ethnic groups. The Tosks make up a majority in southern Albania, while the Gegs dominate the north. Here, a Tosk and his grandson rest in the courtyard of a church.

17

Passengers leave a train at the central station of Durres. Albania's small network of railways includes 316 miles of track and links Durres with Shkoder, Elbasan, and Tirane.

Shkoder from a rocky outcropping, has been occupied by Illyrians, Romans, Venetians, and Ottoman Turks. The residents of Shkoder rebuilt many of its buildings after a strong earthquake in 1979. One of the city's main attractions is the Museum of Atheism, which Albania's Communist government built to celebrate its ban on all forms of religious practice.

The port of Vlore (population 77,000) faces the wide Bay of Vlore in southern Albania. Many of the nation's exports and imports pass through this city, which lies about 40 miles from Italy across the Strait of Otranto. To promote tourism, the government is planning new resorts along the Adriatic coast south of Vlore.

The traditional red-tiled homes of Gjirokaster, a hill town of southern Albania, offer a pleasant contrast to the factories and drab concrete apartments in many larger Albanian cities. Cobblestoned streets wind between Gjirokaster's tall, whitewashed houses. In 1961 the government passed a decree banning new construction in the town, which is also famous as the birthplace of the Albanian Communist leader Enver Hoxha.

Many Albanians spend their free time chatting with friends and acquaintances in small cafes.

The remains of a Greek temple stand at Apollonia, an ancient settlement near the Adriatic Sea. The ancient Greeks built several ports in southern Albania and traded with the Illyrians, who lived in the Balkan Peninsula of southern Europe.

Photo by Frank Jossi

2) History and Government

Modern Albanians are descended from the ancient Illyrians, who moved into the Balkan Peninsula from northern Europe around 1000 B.C. The Illyrians built self-governing cities throughout the western Balkans. They traded with other peoples of the region and with cities on the Italian Peninsula.

In the sixth century B.C., Greek settlers from Corfu established ports on the Adriatic coast at Apollonia (near modern Vlore) and farther north at Epidamnus (modern Durres). But the Illyrians living in Al-

bania's rugged mountains resisted Greek settlement. Illyrian raiders attacked the coastal cities, and Illyrian pirates threatened Greek trading ships in the Adriatic Sea. Nevertheless, Albania remained a valuable prize for states seeking control of trade in the Balkans and along the Adriatic coast.

Illyria and Rome

Bardhyl, who ruled the Illyrians after 383 B.C., fought with Greek settlers and

The rocky heights above Shkoder form a strategic defensive position that has been occupied for thousands of years. The Fortress of Rozafa and other strongholds on the steep hill protected the city from invasion by sea and by land.

Courtesy of Illyria, The Albanian-American Newspaper, NY

with Macedonia, a powerful Greek realm to the southeast. In the third century B.C., the Illyrian king Agron united many independent cities and greatly expanded Illyrian territory. Agron made Shkoder his capital and built an army and navy to protect Illyrian cities and ports.

After Agron's death in 231 B.C., Illyria passed to his widow Teuta. The queen ordered several attacks on neighboring states. But the raids of Illyrian pirates in the Adriatic Sea made Teuta's realm an enemy of Rome, a powerful and growing state on the Italian Peninsula. Roman

Photo by Zamir Marika

Thousands of tiny stones make up this mosaic floor, which survives in Durres. This city has been a busy port for more than 2,000 years. The ancient Romans—who called the city Durrachium—used the port as a link to their colonies on the Balkan Peninsula.

Photo by Zamir Marika

Early Christians built the Saint Thanasi Basilica near Korce. After the fall of the Roman Empire, Albania came under the control of the Byzantine (or Eastern Roman) Empire, which was also the center of the eastern Christian church.

troops defeated Teuta's army and seized the port of Epidamnus, which the Romans renamed Durrachium.

In 168 B.C., Rome added what is now Albania to its province of Illyricum, which covered the western Balkan Peninsula. Skilled Roman engineers extended the Via Egnatia, an old Illyrian road, all the way from Durrachium to Constantinople. The Via Egnatia became a vital route for Balkan trade and for Roman troops sent to guard Rome's Balkan territories.

Around A.D. 10, the Romans began recruiting Illyrian soldiers into the Roman army. These troops were needed to defend the empire from the raids of northern European peoples, who were attacking Roman towns and outposts in central Europe.

The Illyrians were famous for their fighting skill and discipline, and several Illyrian military leaders rose through the ranks to become Roman emperors. Yet many Illyrian groups, such as the Albanoi (from whom Albania takes its name), continued to resist Roman rule. Living in the rugged and inaccessible Balkan mountains, these groups held fast to their ancient customs and to their independence.

Byzantine Rule

As raids from northern Europe continued and as the empire began to suffer political turmoil, Rome lost control of its provinces. In A.D. 395, the empire split into western and eastern halves. This event also caused an important division within Albania. While the northern Albanians remained under Roman influence, the people of southern Albania forged closer links with the Greek peoples to the south.

Devastated by an attack of the Goths, a nomadic group from northern Europe, the Western Roman Empire collapsed in the fifth century. The Eastern or Byzantine Empire survived with its capital at Constantinople. The Byzantine emperors, who ruled Greece as well as Albania, fought

21

against the Goths and against other peoples for control of the Balkan Peninsula.

At the same time, Christianity—which had become Rome's official religion—was also going through important changes. Christian leaders in Rome and Constantinople disagreed over the beliefs and ceremonies of their faith. This led to a split within the church. Constantinople became the center of an eastern, or Orthodox, branch of Christianity, while Rome remained the capital of the western, or Roman Catholic, church.

Loyalty to these two branches followed the division of Albania into northern and southern regions. The people of northern Albania remained within the Roman Catholic Church, while most southerners adopted Orthodox Christianity.

Northern Invaders

The Balkan Peninsula continued to suffer attacks by nomadic peoples of northern and eastern Europe. The Goths and Huns plundered the cities, homes, and fields of the Illyrians. The Slavs of eastern Europe invaded between 570 and 640. After settling much of the Balkans and intermarrying with the inhabitants, the Slavs introduced their language and culture to the region. But they were not strong enough to conquer the people of Albania, whose ancient communities evolved into fiercely independent clans (groups of families).

Albania remained an isolated place where landowning families ruled over large, private domains. Small principalities (realms of princes) developed near port cities and

Courtesy of Italian Government Tourist Bureau

In the A.D. 530s, the Byzantine emperor Justinian (center) extended a new law code, based on the ancient Roman law, to all the empire's territories, including Albania.

in fertile river valleys. In the mountains, the Albanian clans fought for territory and for scarce natural resources.

In the mid-ninth century, the Bulgars, who had moved into Europe from central Asia, set up a Bulgarian kingdom in the eastern Balkans. The Bulgarian leader Simeon I defeated the Byzantine army and established colonies along the Adriatic seacoast. Shishman, who succeeded Simeon, conquered Durres, the former Roman port of Durrachium that still traded with cities in Greece and Italy.

But the Byzantine emperor Basil II, nicknamed the "Bulgar-slayer," counter-attacked in 1014. The Byzantine forces smashed the Bulgarian army, seized the Adriatic ports, and conquered Epirus, which lies south of Albania.

These territories were far from the Byzantine capital at Constantinople, however, and Byzantine authority in the area gradually weakened. While the clans and landowners controlled the countryside, the people of the coastal cities fought against Byzantine rule. It was during this period of rebellion and turmoil that the region first came to be known as Albania.

The ports of Albania remained a valuable prize for several rival nations. The Normans, who ruled a kingdom in southern Italy, conquered Durres in 1081. The wealthy trading city of Venice, in northern Italy, built fortresses and trading posts in Albania's lowlands.

Divided into warring clans, the Albanians were unable to prevent the occupation of their country by outsiders. In 1272 Charles d'Anjou, the ruler of the Kingdom of Naples and Sicily, attacked from his base in southern Italy. Charles conquered Durres and much of central Albania. Charles called his new domain the Kingdom of Albania.

By this time, Serbia, a realm to the northeast, had already established a dynasty (family of rulers) at Shkoder to take control of northern Albania. In the mid-1300s, Stephen Dushan, a powerful Serbian

Photo by The Bodleian Library, Oxford MS.Bodl. 264, fol. 218r

With a powerful fleet and far-flung colonies, the Italian city of Venice grew rich from trade in the Mediterranean Sea. The Venetians built several trading posts in Albania and, in the fifteenth century, controlled Shkoder and Durres.

prince, conquered much of the western Balkans. Dushan drew up a legal code for his realm and crowned himself "Emperor of the Serbs, Greeks, Bulgarians, and Albanians." But in 1355, while leading an attack against Constantinople, Dushan suddenly died. His empire quickly broke apart.

The constant warfare in Albania was causing poverty and deadly famines. Beginning in the fourteenth century, many Albanians left their troubled homeland and migrated southward into the mountains of Epirus and to the cities and islands of Greece. Albanian exiles also built communities in southern Italy and on the island of Sicily.

Turkish Conquest

The political chaos in Albania allowed several noble families to establish powerful private domains. In the 1360s, as the Serbs withdrew from the north, the Ballsha dynasty took control of Shkoder and the northern highlands. Thirty years later, the cities of Durres and Kruje fell to the

For more than five centuries, Skanderbeg has been the national hero of the Albanians. Before his death from malaria in 1468, he never lost a battle to the Turks. But feuds among Skanderbeg's successors weakened their resistance to the powerful Ottoman armies. By the mid-sixteenth century, most of Albania was under Turkish rule.

Courtesy of Albanian Catholic Bulletin

Kastrioti dynasty. The Dukagjin family ruled Lezhe and nearby territory in the Albanian lowlands.

Conflict among these dynasties soon led to civil war. The fighting weakened Albania's defenses at a time when the powerful Ottoman Empire was expanding into the Balkans. In 1389 the Turks crushed a combined force of Albanians, Serbians, Bulgarians, Romanians, and Hungarians at Kosovo, a plain lying northeast of Albania. This victory allowed the Ottoman Empire to occupy much of the Balkan Peninsula.

In the early 1400s, the Ottomans invaded Epirus and began moving north toward Albania. The squabbling Albanian dynasties could not unite to resist the Turks, who quickly overran the region. To rule these lands, the Turks offered control of *pashaliks* (Ottoman provinces) to the Albanian landowners. In return the landowners had to pledge their loyalty to the Ottoman sultan (ruler).

Turkish rule did not extend into the rugged highlands, where many Albanian clans preserved their laws and independence. In the mid-1400s, the Albanian prince Lek Dukagjini compiled a system of traditional laws known as "The Canon of Lek Dukagjini." For centuries the elders of the clans passed on this code by word of mouth, using it to resolve disputes and to punish wrongdoing.

SKANDERBEG'S BATTLES

During the Ottoman attacks, the Turks had captured Georgi Kastrioti, the young heir of the wealthy Kastrioti clan. Like many other young Albanian hostages, he was brought to the Ottoman capital of Istanbul, where he was given military training and instructed in the Islamic faith, the religion of the Turks.

Under Sultan Murad II, Kastrioti became a high-ranking officer in the Ottoman army. After fighting many battles for the Turks, Kastrioti received the name Iskander (Alexander) and the honorary title of *bey* ("lord" in the Turkish language). In the Albanian language, these names became Skanderbeg.

In 1443 Skanderbeg abandoned Islam, raised a force of 12,000 Albanian soldiers, and began attacking the sultan's army. In the next year, he established a fortified headquarters at Kruje, the Kastrioti stronghold in central Albania, and organized a league of Albanian princes to fight for independence. Skanderbeg turned back more than a dozen Turkish invasions before decisively defeating Murad's armies in 1450.

After Skanderbeg fell ill and died in 1468, the Turks again attacked Albania. This time the Ottoman Empire occupied Kruje and completely defeated the Albanian armies. Durres fell in 1502, and within a few decades only the most isolated highlands of Albania remained free of Turkish control.

Ottoman Rule

After their victory, the Turks imposed heavy taxes on Albanians and seized the property of those who would not convert to Islam. Albanian Muslims (followers of Islam) ruled the pashaliks as the sultan's chosen representatives. Frequent

Photo by Picture Collection, The Branch Libraries, The New York Public Library

Turks and Albanians clash during the struggle over control of the Balkan Peninsula. The Ottoman Empire took advantage of disunity among the Balkan states and occupied the region until the early twentieth century.

quarreling among these rulers prevented them from making alliances to defy the Turkish forces.

Christians were excluded from government posts, and many Albanians accepted Islam in order to join the Turkish civil service. Some of them became *pashas,* or governors, of other Ottoman territories. Some became soldiers and officers in the Turkish army. Within Albania Muslims opened schools and founded an academy that competed with Europe's Christian universities.

By the late eighteenth century, however, the huge Ottoman Empire was in decline. The Turkish administration grew inefficient and corrupt, and rival states began fighting for Ottoman territory. In Albania the most powerful landowning families were exercising more power than the sultan. Mehmet Bey, leader of the pashalik of Shkoder, united the towns of northern Albania and established the independent Bushati dynasty.

Meanwhile, Ali Pasha, the Albanian ruler of the town of Tepelene, was fighting a guerrilla war against Russia, an empire of eastern Europe that was expanding into the Balkans. In 1800 Ali Pasha forged an independent domain along the entire Albanian coast, from Greece and Epirus in the south to Montenegro in the north.

Under Ali Pasha's leadership, his capital of Ioannina in Epirus grew in wealth and population and became a political center of southeastern Europe. To help their interests in the region, Britain and France sent diplomats to Ioannina and set up consulates in the city. But the sultan, who was jealous and fearful of Ali Pasha's growing power, ordered a huge force to attack Ioannina in 1819. Three years later, after overthrowing Ali Pasha's empire, the Turks captured and executed him.

Courtesy of Cultural and Tourism Office of the Turkish Embassy

Ali Pasha built this palace on the banks of Lake Ioannina in Epirus, in what is now northern Greece. Ruler of Albania and western Greece, he wrested his independence from the Turkish sultan (ruler) and allied himself with powerful western European countries. But in 1822, the Turks attacked Ioannina, captured Ali Pasha, and quickly executed him.

Wearing traditional clothing, Albanians relax at an outdoor cafe in Shkoder in the early 1900s. Shkoder became the first city to openly rebel against Turkish rule.

The Drive for Independence

In response to these events, Turkish rulers created a new legal system that increased the sultan's authority throughout Albania. But the Albanians and several other Balkan peoples opposed these changes, and revolt swept through the region.

European states saw this rebellion, and the decline of the Ottoman Empire, as an opportunity to expand their power. Russia sought control of ports in southern Europe. The Russians also aimed to win allies among the Balkan peoples who were fighting the Turks. Britain, which controlled a worldwide empire, wanted to seize Turkish territory and stop Russian expansion. Italy and Austria—a central European empire—battled one another for strategic towns and forts on the Adriatic coast.

In 1877, after defeating Ottoman forces in the Balkans, Russia forced Turkey to sign the Treaty of San Stefano. This and

Albanian rebels smuggle arms and ammunition into the country during an uprising against the country's Turkish occupiers. Many weapons were brought into the region by Russia, which sought to end Turkish control of the Balkan Peninsula.

27

A painting by the Albanian artist Nexhmedin Zajmi shows uniformed soldiers talking with peasants during the Balkan conflicts of the early twentieth century.

other agreements granted independence to several Balkan nations. The treaties also turned over Balkan territories with large Albanian populations to Austria, Serbia, Greece, and Montenegro.

These actions prompted Albanian clan leaders to form the Albanian League. The members vowed to fight against the division of their nation by stronger European powers. The league also sought to win more freedom for Albanians still living under Ottoman rule.

At first the Turkish government supported the league. The Ottoman leaders hoped to use the organization to undermine the treaties and to stop Austria and Italy from seizing land in the Balkans. But when the Albanian League succeeded in winning back territory from Montenegro, the sultan began to fear Albanian demands for independence. In 1880 the Turkish army attacked and defeated the military arm of the Albanian League, forcing the league to disband.

Despite their loss of territory in the Balkans, the Turks were determined to keep control of Albania. To achieve this goal, the Turkish government completely banned Albanian writings, public schooling, and the use of the Albanian language. In response to these harsh measures, many Albanians emigrated in search of education and jobs.

Nevertheless, as the Ottoman Empire continued to weaken, the drive for freedom survived. Albanian nationalists published their writings abroad and sought help for their cause in Europe and in the United States. They also found allies among members of the Turkish government.

In the early 1900s, a group of Turkish politicians known as the Young Turks sought to prevent the empire's further decline by making changes in the Ottoman administration. They proposed political and economic reforms that would have lessened the absolute powers of the sultan. But the Albanians rejected a new constitution written by the Young Turks. This move sparked an open revolt against Turkish rule.

In 1909 Albanians serving in the Ottoman army mutinied. During the next two years, Albanian independence fighters attacked Turkish forces in Shkoder and Kosovo. In March 1911, rebels forced the Turks to retreat from Albania's northern highlands. For the first time in centuries, Albanian fighters raised the traditional banner of Skanderbeg, which they adopted as the new Albanian flag.

Unable to stem the revolt, the Turkish government granted self-rule to several Albanian provinces. On November 28, 1912, Albanian leaders met in Vlore to declare their country's independence. Ismail Qemali, an Albanian member of the Turkish parliament, became the head of an independent Albanian government.

Turmoil in the Balkans

As Ottoman power continued to decline, the Balkan Peninsula became a chaotic battleground of competing states and ethnic groups. Serbia, Montenegro, and Greece fought one another for Albanian territory. The Albanians, who were still divided among competing clans and political groups, were unable to agree on a common strategy for their young nation.

Stronger European states—including Britain, France, Germany, Austria, and Italy (also known as the Great Powers)— sought to resolve these conflicts to their own advantage. To reach their goal, the leaders of these nations redrew Albania's borders and tried to dictate the new nation's form of government.

In July 1913, at an international conference, the Great Powers agreed to recognize Albanian independence. Ambassadors at the conference drew up a new constitution for Albania, decreed that the nation would become a hereditary monarchy, and nominated the German prince Wilhelm zu Wied as the first king.

To settle the competing territorial claims, a commission then set down Albania's new boundaries. The borders excluded ethnic Albanians in several neighboring countries. As a result, Montenegro, Macedonia, northern Greece, and Kosovo— which became part of Serbia—now had

The London Conference of 1913 fixed new boundaries for Albania and for other nations that had recently thrown off Turkish occupation. But the settlement also left many Albanians living in neighboring countries—including Montenegro and Serbia—and led to conflicts that continue to the present day.

Artwork by Laura Westlund

large Albanian communities living outside their homeland.

The withdrawal of the Ottoman Empire did not bring peace to Albania. Greek attacks in the south and a revolt against the foreign-appointed monarchy brought violence and social turmoil. Rival clans clashed over territory, and landowners fought among themselves for influence in the new government. After Wilhelm zu Wied's arrival in March 1914, Essad Pasha—the successor of Ismail Qemali—denounced the German monarch and formed a rebel army. Essad Pasha had the support of Italy, which now saw Albania as an important ally on the Balkan Peninsula.

WORLD WAR I

Conflict in other parts of the Balkans led to the outbreak of World War I in 1914. In the next year, Germany and Austria allied with the Ottoman Empire to fight France, Britain, Russia, and Italy. As foreign armies mobilized along Albania's borders and as opposition to his reign increased, Wilhelm zu Wied fled the country.

During World War I, seven foreign nations battled for Albanian territory. Greece attacked in the south, Italy occupied Vlore, and the French took control of the Korce Basin. The armies of Austria, Montenegro, Bulgaria, and Serbia also marched into the country to seize land and to fight one another.

After Germany's surrender in November 1918 ended World War I, representatives of the victorious nations met in Paris to redraw the map of Europe. But the ambassadors found themselves unable to agree on Albania's borders. Greece claimed southern Albania, while Italy still occu-

Artwork by Laura Westlund

The modern Albanian flag carries the two-headed eagle, the symbol of Skanderbeg. An old tradition claims that the first Albanians were descended from an eagle.

Photo © Massimo Sciacca

The Turks did not allow public education in Albania. After independence and World War I, the Albanian government founded new primary and secondary schools. The educational system expanded further after World War II, but many schools, including this high school in Tirane, still have a shortage of books and other materials.

pied Vlore. Serbia and Montenegro were demanding sections of northern Albania.

Angry at this foreign interference, Albanian leaders convened their own conference at Lushnje in January 1920. They again declared their country's independence and named Tirane as the new Albanian capital. Ahmet Zogu, a politician and landowner, organized a national defense force. That summer Zogu's fighters drove Italian troops out of Vlore and brought the foreign occupation of Albania to an end.

The Republic and King Zog

After the war, Albanians struggled to establish a modern government and to reform the nation's ancient system of hereditary landownership. But the reformers were strongly opposed by conservatives who fought against change in Albania's legal and economic systems. Ahmet Zogu, who was elected prime minister in 1922,

became the leader of the conservative faction.

In 1924 a popular revolt forced Zogu to flee to Yugoslavia, a union of Balkan republics that was formed after World War I. The fall of Zogu's government allowed Fan Noli, an Orthodox bishop, to organize a new Albanian administration.

Although he sought to reform the Albanian economy and to bring in new investment, Noli was unable to attract foreign aid. Conservatives weakened his programs by strongly opposing his government. Noli also angered Albania's landowners by recognizing the Soviet Union, a Communist nation established by Russian revolutionaries. By late 1924, conflict among political parties had paralyzed the Albanian legislature. In December Ahmet Zogu returned at the head of an army and overthrew Bishop Noli.

With little opposition, Zogu declared himself the president of a new Albanian republic. He signed military treaties with Italy, which promised to protect Albania from invasion or further division. In 1928, under pressure from the president, the legislature created a hereditary monarchy. Ahmet Zogu became King Zog I.

With financial support from Italy, the new king planned to modernize Albania. The government again attempted to break up some of the large private estates, and a bank was set up to assist Albanian farmers. Zog also ordered the construction of new roads, port facilities, and industries.

But King Zog's alliance with Italy soon brought trouble. The Italian dictator Benito Mussolini saw Albania not as an ally but as a valuable colony for his own country. In return for financial aid, Mussolini demanded the establishment of Italian communities in Albania and the teaching of Italian in Albanian schools. By these actions, he hoped to make Albania more dependent on Italy.

During the 1930s, Zog's close ties with Mussolini sparked protests among Albanians who feared an Italian takeover of their country. The king's strict rule also gave rise to an opposition movement of Albanian Communists. This group worked underground, in alliance with the Soviet Union, to overthrow King Zog and to establish a socialist state, in which the government would control Albanian farms, mines, and industries.

Occupation and War

Meanwhile, events in the rest of Europe were again leading to a world war. The dictator Adolf Hitler took power in Germany, strengthened his nation's military, and formed an alliance with Mussolini. Germany and Italy began planning the conquest of Europe, including the Balkan region.

In April 1939, Italian troops attacked Albania and forced King Zog to flee to Greece.

Photo by Zamir Marika

Before World War II, Enver Hoxha studied in France and also worked as a diplomat in Belgium. Although he traveled much more widely than most Albanian leaders, he was suspicious of foreign influence. After he became Albania's leader, he cut all ties with western Europe.

A Greek gun crew readies a bombardment in southern Albania during World War II. Greeks and Albanians fought Italy and Germany during the war, but Greece occupied part of Albania to claim territory along a disputed border.

Italy occupied Tirane and took control of Albania's administration and economy. Later that year, Germany invaded Poland and touched off World War II.

Although Mussolini ordered an attack on northern Greece in the fall of 1940, the Greeks threw back the Italian forces. Greek and Yugoslavian troops then marched into the Albanian towns of Korce, Gjirokaster, and Sarande. But in the spring of 1941, Germany came to Italy's aid by attacking and occupying Albania and Greece.

As the war continued, Albanians formed resistance groups to harass the Italian and German occupation forces. Meanwhile, in 1941, opponents of the prewar Albanian government had organized an Albanian Communist party under the leadership of Enver Hoxha. Communist guerrillas and members of the Balli Kombetar, an anti-

Communist group, joined forces to fight the occupation.

When Mussolini fell from power in 1943, Italy withdrew from Albania. After a series of fierce battles, the Germans were driven from the country in November 1944. With the tide turning against Germany, the Albanian resistance groups began fighting one another for control of Albania's postwar government. The conflict worsened the damages already suffered by Albania. By the end of World War II in 1945, nearly one-third of the nation's housing, livestock, and farms had been destroyed.

Communist Victories

With the support of Yugoslavia's Communist party, Hoxha established a provisional (temporary) Albanian government. The

33

Photo © Massimo Sciacca

nation's Communists—became the only legal political organization. Hoxha cut off trade and diplomatic relations with western Europe and allied Albania closely with Joseph Stalin, the head of the Soviet Union.

Using Stalin's regime as a model, Albania's rulers began the transformation of their own country into a strict socialist state. The government seized property and land and became the sole employer of farmers, miners, and factory workers. Private ownership of businesses, shops, homes, and automobiles became illegal.

Hoxha used financial aid from the Soviet Union to improve Albania's schools, hospitals, and transportation systems. Once a largely agricultural country with only a few factories, Albania quickly built new industries. Eventually, nearly half of the population worked in manufacturing, mining, or construction.

Albania also formed new business ventures with Yugoslavia. But when Josip Broz Tito, the ruler of Yugoslavia, threw

anti-Communist groups, which were splintered into several feuding factions, were easily defeated by the Communists in the first postwar elections in late 1945.

Hoxha, the first secretary (leader) of the party, renamed his country the People's Republic of Albania. The Albanian Party of Labor—the official name adopted by the

This five-pointed star, an important symbol of Albania's Communist regime, marks the entrance to a now-abandoned factory.

Photo © 1991 Jim Stone

Photo by Frank Jossi

The Soviet Union, a powerful Communist state, helped Albania improve its transportation network in the 1950s. Soviet advisers, engineers, and technicians designed many new railway lines and highway routes.

his support to one of Hoxha's political rivals, Hoxha turned against his neighbor. In the late 1940s, Albania and Yugoslavia broke off relations.

In 1955 Albania agreed to join the Warsaw Pact, a military alliance of Communist nations led by the Soviet Union. To help Albania's rapid industrialization, Soviet leaders sent advisers, equipment, and financial aid. Under production goals set by the government, new factories in Albania's cities assembled heavy equipment and other products for export to other Warsaw Pact countries.

The Policy of Isolation

After Stalin died in 1953, many Albanian Communists called for changes in the Stalinist system that Hoxha had adopted.

Courtesy of Illyria, The Albanian-American Newspaper, NY

The parliament building in Tirane carries the Albanian state seal.

But Hoxha resisted these demands, seeing in them a threat to his own authority. To fight the pressure for reform, he further isolated his country from the Soviet Union. Hoxha criticized Nikita Khrushchev, Stalin's successor, and arrested rivals who supported Khrushchev's reforms. To Albania's leader, it seemed that Khrushchev was destroying Stalin's accomplishments and straying from true socialism.

In 1961 the Soviet Union and China—the world's two largest Communist nations—fell into a disagreement over their economic and foreign policies. The Chinese leader Mao Zedong, like Hoxha, strongly opposed Khrushchev's reforms. When Albania announced its support of China in this dispute, Khrushchev broke off relations with Albania. Soviet and Albanian forces nearly clashed over control of a Soviet submarine base in Vlore.

The Soviet Union abandoned the base but also cut off aid and removed all Soviet-supplied equipment from Albania. Factories in Tirane and other cities were left without machinery or spare parts. To stop an economic decline, Albania then allied with China, which sent equipment and advisers to help Albanian industries improve their production during the 1960s.

In 1968, after the Soviet Union crushed a revolt in the Warsaw Pact nation of Czechoslovakia, Hoxha withdrew his country from the alliance. As Albania grew increasingly isolated, Hoxha also began cracking down on opposition within his own country. Albania's secret police imprisoned thousands of people suspected of disloyalty to the government. The regime also announced that Albania would become an atheistic state (one without religion). Security forces arrested Muslim and Christian clergy, banned public worship, and closed all churches and mosques.

Albania broke with China in the early 1970s after China opened diplomatic relations with the United States, a country

Courtesy of Illyria, The Albanian-American Newspaper, NY

Bunkers line a pasture outside an Albanian village. Hoxha ordered hundreds of thousands of the bunkers to be built. But instead of conflict with western Europe or the United States, Albania nearly went to war with the Soviet Union in the early 1960s after the two nations ended their close alliance.

Ramiz Alia became the leader of Albania after the death of Enver Hoxha in 1985. Unlike Hoxha, Alia allowed trade with foreign countries. Nevertheless, Albania's economy continued to weaken.

Photo by Albanian Telegraphic Agency

that Hoxha considered a dangerous enemy. In 1978 China stopped all military and financial aid to Albania. Hoxha's government was left without allies among Communist or non-Communist nations.

Determined to seal off their country from foreign influences, Albania's leaders made it illegal to travel abroad, to read foreign books or magazines, or to listen to foreign radio broadcasts. Visitors could not enter the country, and trade with the outside world was forbidden. Fearing an invasion from the United States or western Europe, Hoxha ordered the construction of more than 800,000 fortified concrete bunkers in the countryside.

The ban on trade and foreign investment greatly harmed Albania's economy, and Hoxha's harsh policies also fostered opposition within his own government. In 1981 prime minister Mehmet Shehu called for increased foreign trade with non-Communist nations. But in December, after coming under sharp criticism from Hoxha, Shehu suddenly died.

Although the government called the death a suicide, many Albanians believed that Hoxha had ordered his prime minister's execution. After Shehu's death, the secret police arrested and killed many members of the government who agreed with Shehu's views. In the early 1980s, as Hoxha's health began to fail, he supported Ramiz Alia, a close friend and ally, as his successor.

Recent Events

After Enver Hoxha died in April 1985, the post of first secretary passed to Alia. Under his leadership, Albania gradually changed its economic policies and established diplomatic ties with more than 100 countries. Albania also began exporting some of its mineral resources, especially chromium.

Despite these changes, factory production fell, and the country continued its slide into economic depression. The ban on travel and on reading foreign books continued, and thousands of political prisoners remained under arrest. With their living standards falling rapidly, many Albanians demanded change.

In 1989 failing economies also sparked public demonstrations in the other Communist nations of Europe. For the first time since World War II, Warsaw Pact countries held free elections, some of which led to the defeat of Soviet-allied Communists. In addition, several of the republics that made up Yugoslavia declared their independence, leading to a civil war.

In Albania Ramiz Alia eased restrictions on travel and allowed citizens to own private homes. He freed most political prisoners, gave state-owned businesses some independence, and lifted the ban on religious practice. For the first time since World War II, Albania sought financial aid from non-Communist nations.

These measures were not enough to stem the rising tide of opposition to Albania's Communist government. Violent anti-government demonstrations broke out in Shkoder, and a mob in Tirane destroyed a prominent statue of Enver Hoxha. In 1990, as the turmoil continued, thousands of Albanians stormed foreign embassies in the capital to seek asylum (protection) abroad. Many others fled southward to Greece and across the Adriatic Sea to Italy.

To stop the violence, the Albanian Party of Labor legalized opposition parties and called for open elections. The government renamed the country the Republic of Albania and drew up a new constitution, which established an elected presidency.

The Democratic Party of Albania—the largest opposition group—rallied thousands of students, farmers, and townspeople to its ranks. In 1992, after winning a majority in the Albanian legislature, the party took power. Sali Berisha, the party's leader, became Albania's president.

The new government of Albania has lifted all travel and trade restrictions. Albania is also selling state-owned factories and mining operations to private investors. Farmers now grow crops on their own acreages and are free to sell their produce on the open market.

Nevertheless, Albania's economy is still weak, and the country's living standards remain the lowest in Europe. Factories have closed, unemployment is rising, and many Albanians want to emigrate. The country is seeking foreign aid and private investment to rebuild its industries. To join the European trading economy, the new government is working to overcome Albania's long isolation from the rest of the continent.

Government

The Albanian government is a parliamentary democracy. The 140 members of the

A shopowner in Durres proudly stands among his colorful inventory of jackets and dresses. The new government of Albania permits private shops, which the Communist regime banned.

Members of the Albanian legislature meet in the parliament building in downtown Tirane. In the background is the Albanian coat of arms, which the Albanian Communist party designed after World War II.

Photo © Massimo Sciacca

judges the constitutionality of new laws and resolves disputes within the administration. Albania is now training private attorneys—whom the Communists banned from practicing—to represent defendants in Albania's courts.

Albania has 26 administrative districts, 42 municipalities, and 304 rural communities known as communes. Each city, town, or village has a local governmental body that enforces laws passed by the administrative districts. The municipalities elect their local officials and councils to three-year terms.

People's Assembly—the Albanian legislature—serve four-year terms. Each of the nation's 100 legislative districts has a single representative. The remaining 40 members of the assembly are "at-large" members who do not represent a specific city or region. The constitution allows each political party a certain number of at-large members, based on the percentage of votes the party receives in national elections.

The assembly has the power to rewrite the constitution, to pass laws, to draw up a national budget, and to confirm or revoke the president's decision to declare war. Every five years, the legislature elects a president to serve as the government's head of state. The president nominates the chairperson of the Council of Ministers, which includes the heads of the government's 14 ministries.

After the fall of its Communist regime, Albania reformed its judicial system. The members of the Supreme Court, the nation's highest court, are elected by the People's Assembly. District courts and appeals courts hear civil and criminal cases. A new constitutional court of nine members

Courtesy of Aramco World

The leader of the Democratic Party of Albania, Sali Berisha, became the nation's president in 1992.

Schoolchildren crowd around a street vendor offering chestnuts in Tirane. The painting behind the students is in the socialist-realism style, which celebrated social progress made under Albania's former government.

Courtesy of Illyria, The Albanian-American Newspaper, NY

3) The People

About 97 percent of Albania's 3.3 million people are ethnic Albanians, who trace their language and culture back to the ancient Illyrians. Albania also is home to Romanians, Bulgarians, and Serbs. Ethnic Greeks inhabit several villages near the country's border with Greece. Gypsies, a nomadic people who live throughout the Balkan region, make up a small percentage of Albania's population.

The agreement of 1913, which set Albania's modern boundaries, left half of the Albanian population in foreign lands. More than two million Albanians now live in Macedonia and Montenegro (formerly parts of Yugoslavia) and in Kosovo, a semi-independent region of Serbia.

Although Albania's cities have grown rapidly since the end of World War II, nearly two-thirds of the people still reside in rural towns and villages. The country's worsening economy has shut down many factories, driving some Albanians out of the country altogether. After travel restrictions were lifted in the late 1980s, thousands of Albanians emigrated to western Europe, especially to Italy and Germany, and to the United States.

Ethnic Heritage

Ethnic Albanians were the only Balkan people to resist conquest by the Slavs, who invaded the peninsula in the sixth and seventh centuries A.D. As a result, Albanians remain closely related to their Illyrian ancestors. In addition, the Albanian language is a unique branch of the Indo-European language family, which now dominates Europe.

There are two distinct groups of ethnic Albanians. The Tosks dwell mainly south

A girl carries her young brother through the streets of Elbasan.

of the Shkumbin River, and the Gegs live in the north. The mountain strongholds of northern Albania allowed the Gegs to resist foreign rule, but the Tosks—most of whom farmed river valleys and coastal plains—absorbed the ideas and cultures of several foreign invaders.

The traditional clan system of Albania survived until the mid-1900s, despite centuries of invasion, division, and occupation. The typical Albanian clan, or *bajrak*, included several families who shared their land and possessions. The clan's leader was known as a *bajraktar*. The elders of

Although this family has few possessions, it can enjoy programs of the national television station, which broadcasts from the capital.

A laborer rests in a field near the port of Durres. Lacking modern equipment, many Albanian farm workers must cultivate their fields with simple tools.

the clan used the code of Lek Dukagjini, a fifteenth-century prince, to settle disputes. Women remained inside the home and could not inherit property. In addition, parents arranged all marriages.

Clan society changed rapidly in the years after World War II. Industrialization attracted rural Albanians to urban centers in search of better living conditions, and for the first time Albanian women entered the labor force. The seizure of farmland by the Communist government broke up many of the bajraks, whose members were forced to work on state-owned collective farms.

Photo © Massimo Sciacca

Photo © Massimo Sciacca

This Catholic church is one of the few religious buildings left standing in Elbasan. Most of the city's churches and mosques were destroyed or converted to other uses after World War II.

Muslims attend a prayer service in an Albanian mosque. Most Albanians follow the Islamic faith, which was brought to the region by the Muslim Turks.

Nevertheless, in isolated rural areas—and especially in northern Albania—some families remain loyal to their clans. Among strongly traditional families, women have little freedom to work outside the home, and parents still select the marriage partners of their children.

Religion

Under Communist rule, few Albanians dared to openly practice their religion. The government closed religious buildings or converted them into homes, warehouses, or sports centers. In 1967 Enver Hoxha outlawed religion entirely, creating the world's first officially atheist state. During the ban, the country's religious leaders suffered imprisonment, exile, and execution.

Worshipers as well as tourists visit this Orthodox church near Berat.

Many Albanians worshiped in private, however, and religious faith survived. In May 1990, during the presidency of Ramiz Alia, the legislature reversed Hoxha's decree. Soon Muslims and Christians were opening schools, holding services, and attracting new converts.

More than 70 percent of Albanians belong to the Islamic faith, a religion founded in the seventh century A.D. by the prophet Muhammad. The Islamic Turks brought this faith to Albania during the Ottoman conquest of the Balkan Peninsula. Most Albanian Muslims are Sunnis, a sect that accepts Islamic leaders who are not descended from Muhammad's family. Others are Shiites, who only follow leaders descended from Muhammad's family.

The Bektashi are members of a modern Islamic sect that was forced out of Turkey in the early 1900s. Elbasan, Berat, and several cities of southern Albania are home to many Bektashi Muslims, who have made Albania an important center of their faith.

About 20 percent of Albanians, mostly Tosks and ethnic Greeks who live in the south, belong to the Eastern Orthodox Church. For many years after the fall of the Roman Empire, southern Albania was under the control of the Byzantine Empire, an Orthodox state. Roman Catholics, who make up about 10 percent of Albania's population, live in the north, which has historic ties to Rome and to Catholic Italy. In contrast to many other nations of the Balkan region, Christians and Muslims in Albania live together peacefully, often joining in one another's religious observances and celebrations.

Education and Health

Until the 1920s, Albania had no public schools or universities. Ottoman rulers prohibited teaching in the Albanian language, and only a few private Catholic and Turkish schools operated in the cities. Although some schools were founded after independence, nearly 80 percent of the population could not read or write at the start of World War II.

After the war, the Albanian Communist government made universal education an important goal. New laws required all children between the ages of 7 and 15 to attend school. The government built public schools throughout the country but banned private religious instruction. In the early 1990s, the new Albanian government ended this restriction.

Children between the ages of three and six may attend a *kopshte,* or nursery school. At age seven, students begin an eight-year course of studies that includes four years of elementary school and four years of secondary school. Because all students must study other languages, many Albanians can speak one or two

Mother Theresa, whose real name is Agnes Gonxha Bojaxhiu, is one of the world's most famous Albanians. After joining an order of Roman Catholic nuns in 1928, she left for India. In 1950 she founded the Missionaries of Charity, a new Catholic order. Her work with the poor in India earned her the Nobel Peace Prize in 1979.

University students gather during a
classroom break.

foreign tongues, the most common being English and Italian. The modernization of education has also raised the literacy rate in Albania to 90 percent.

The University of Tirane, the nation's first university, opened in 1957. This institution offers degrees in history, economics, medicine, engineering, and other subjects. By the mid-1990s, six other advanced schools had opened. About 75 percent of secondary-school students continue their studies in postsecondary institutes, where students pay tuition based on their family's income.

This building in Korce houses one of the first public schools founded in Albania.

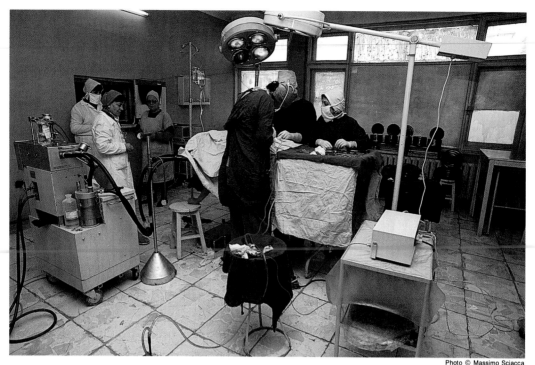

Photo © Massimo Sciacca

Surgeons perform an operation at Tirane's main hospital. Many clinics and hospitals in the country lack important equipment and facilities.

Courtesy of Peace Corps/Michael Honnegar

Villagers stroll along a road in the Albanian countryside.

Albania's health-care system improved after World War II, when the government built several hospitals and opened new training colleges for doctors, dentists, and nurses. All medical services are available at no charge, and medicines are free to children up to one year of age. The state provides health insurance and pensions for workers, as well as financial aid to the unemployed and the disabled.

Despite these changes, the country's health-care system has become outdated. Obsolete equipment hampers treatment, and many regions lack clinics and trained physicians. Life expectancy in Albania has reached 72 years, lower than the figure for Greece but average among the other nations of the Balkan Peninsula. Although Albania has one of the highest birthrates in Europe, the infant mortality rate is also high. In the mid-1990s, the number of babies who died before their first birthday stood at 28 per 1,000 births. In addition, many Albanian children suffer from malnourishment.

Theater, Art, and Music

Albania's Communist government used plays as a method of promoting its policies. Playwrights who were supported by the state had to celebrate the achievements of socialism or the heroic efforts of Albania's World War II guerrilla fighters. The country's first professional theater company began in Shkoder in 1949. Theater companies have since been established in several other Albanian cities.

Artists flourished in Albania despite foreign occupation and frequent warfare. Several pieces by Onufri, a muralist of the sixteenth century, have survived. Kole Idromeno was the most famous artist of the Rilindja movement, a revival of Albanian arts and writing during the nineteenth century. Idromeno used patriotic themes in many of his paintings. After

Photo © Massimo Sciacca

Students work in a studio at the National Academy of Arts in Tirane.

independence the painters Zef Kolombi and Vangjush Mio and the sculptor Odhise Paskali created distinguished works.

In the years following World War II, the government forced artists to use the socialist-realism style, in which laborers and military heroes were commemorated by murals and sculptures in public places. Enver Hoxha appears as a strong and helpful leader in many works of this time. The coming of democracy in the early 1990s allowed Albanian sculptors and painters to begin using cubism, surrealism, and other modern art styles.

Albania has a long and rich tradition of folk music. Epic songs known as *kenge* recall historical events, fables, dreams, and everyday proverbs. Musicians accompany

Courtesy of Aramco World

After World War II, the new Albanian government enlisted artists in a campaign to glorify the nation's leaders. Enver Hoxha became the most common subject for paintings and imposing sculptures.

An Albanian folk group includes singers and musicians who play flutes and the *cifteli*, a stringed instrument. The isolation of the Albanians allowed the nation's folk music to thrive in many of its ancient forms.

the singers with the *lahute*, a stringed instrument, or the *roja*, a wind instrument similar to bagpipes. Folk ensembles called *saze* perform for weddings and other celebrations.

Cesk Zadeja composed the country's first symphony in 1956. Two years later, a full orchestra and a cast of singers staged the first Albanian opera. By the mid-1990s, 20 orchestras were performing in Albania, and a cultural center and an opera house had opened their doors in Tirane.

Language and Literature

The Albanian language, known as *Shqip* to those who speak it, has evolved from the language of the ancient Illyrians. Through contact and conquest, Greek, Latin, Slavic, and Turkish words have been introduced into Albanian. Yet this language has kept a unique system of grammar that is unrelated to that of any other Indo-European tongue. In fact, no standard form of written Albanian existed until the early twentieth century, when the nation officially

The writer Ismail Kadare is well known outside his homeland for *General of the Dead Army* and other novels.

adopted a system of 36 letters based on the ancient Latin alphabet.

Although the Tosks and the Gegs speak separate dialects of Albanian, members of these groups can understand one another. The Geg dialect is also used by ethnic Albanians who live in Montenegro, Kosovo, and Macedonia, while Albanians in Italy and Greece commonly speak Tosk.

The first Albanian writers were Catholic leaders who used the Latin alphabet to transcribe the Albanian language. In 1555 a Catholic priest named Gjon Buzuku compiled a collection of church rituals, creating the first Albanian book. In 1635 Franciscus Blanchus prepared the first dictionary that included Albanian and Latin words.

The drive for Albanian independence in the 1800s sparked the Rilindja movement among Albanian writers. The few Albanians who could read treasured the books of Rilindja historians and poets. These writers used a clear and direct language that could be read aloud and that was easily understood by those who were illiterate.

Sami Bey Frasheri, a leading writer of the nineteenth century, penned a history of Albania as well as the first Albanian stage play. Naim Bey Frasheri, his brother, authored poetry, histories, and schoolbooks. In more than 12,000 verses, Naim Bey's *History of Skanderbeg* describes the life of Albania's national hero.

In the early twentieth century, Faik Konica, a critic, translator, and politician, founded *Albania,* a journal that was distributed throughout western Europe. Bishop Fan Noli, who served as prime minister after Albania's independence, wrote histories of the country and translated the English-language works of Shakespeare, Poe, and Longfellow into Albanian.

The books of Ismail Kadare, Albania's best-known modern author, have been translated into more than 20 languages. His novels include *General of the Dead Army* and *Chronicle in Stone.*

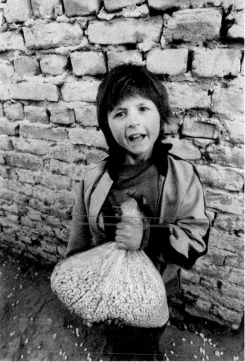

Photo © Massimo Sciacca

In Tirane a boy holds a sack of white beans that will soon be prepared for the family dinner.

Food

Traditional Albanian food has many similarities to Greek and Turkish cuisine. The most popular meat courses are beef, chicken, sausage, and fish. Green and red peppers, cucumbers, and feta (goat or sheep) cheese are often part of the meal. Albanians also enjoy a cheese and bread dish called *byrek.* The mild climate of the Coastal Lowlands allows Albanian farmers to grow many different vegetables and fruits, adding to the variety of foods available to Albanian cooks.

A traditional plate of *meza,* or appetizers, usually offers cheese, olives, cured meats, and sausages. Albanians eat simple main meals that may include salad, meat, pasta, rice, and bread. The national dish, *tave kosi,* consists of lamb, yogurt, eggs, and rice.

Albanians usually drink cups of strong, dark, sweet coffee after meals. Adults also enjoy white and red wines from Durres as well as an after-dinner drink called *raki,* which is made with fermented grapes or plums.

Workers handle molten steel in an Albanian factory. The Communist government invested most of the country's money in heavy industries, and protected these industries from foreign competition. But few manufacturers kept up to date with modern production methods and technology. As a result, obsolete factories cannot compete against western European firms.

4) The Economy

Before World War II, Albania's economy was almost entirely based on agriculture. Albanians depended on Italy and on other neighboring nations for manufactured goods. Only a handful of small industrial plants and workshops existed, and most cities lacked electricity.

Communism transformed Albania's economy. The government took control of farms and businesses and began a system of central planning modeled after the Soviet economy. A series of five-year plans set high production goals for new agricultural collectives, industrial plants, and hydroelectric stations. Roads, bridges, and railroad lines were built. The government's goal was to create a completely self-sufficient nation.

During the 1960s, Albania's industrial production soared, with manufacturing making up about half of the country's output. New railways carried passengers and freight between major cities, and busy hydroelectric plants sold excess electricity

While following a printed pattern, this weaver will tie thousands of small knots with woolen yarn to make a rug. Handcrafted items—such as rugs and musical instruments—have been important Albanian exports since the early 1900s.

to Greece. Albania was exporting oil, designing its own tractors, and producing spare parts for its factories and mines.

Nevertheless, factories often failed to meet their five-year production goals, and during the 1980s the economy stagnated. Wages fell, living standards declined, and a lack of investment quickly made the manufacturing sector obsolete. The falling output of inefficient state-owned farms also forced Albania to import food from Italy and from the Balkan countries. The policy of isolation and self-sufficiency stopped needed aid and investment from Albania's Communist allies.

A young girl watches her goats at a market in Elbasan. Many farmers meet informally to exchange their goods, crops, and livestock.

The riots and strikes of Albania's democratic revolution also caused damage. Factories and state stores closed or were destroyed, leaving Albanians with few sources of consumer goods or food. Prices and unemployment rose, while a lack of trained engineers and technicians hurt the rebuilding effort.

In the early 1990s, the new government began to privatize the economy by selling state-owned farmland and factories. International organizations, such as the World Bank and the International Monetary Fund, made new investments in Albania. Loans from these organizations are helping entrepreneurs to start their own businesses. Farmers also use the aid to buy tractors and other equipment. New stores have opened in Tirane and other cities, and the country's food supply is improving.

Albania is also inviting private foreign companies to make new investments. Firms from western Europe and the United States are funding mining operations and oil exploration. Saudi Arabia, an Islamic kingdom of the Middle East, is helping Albania extract copper. Foreign companies are also interested in developing hotels and tourist resorts on the Adriatic coast. Foreign investment has become a key ingredient in the nation's future growth.

Manufacturing

Albania had almost no manufacturing sector before World War II. After the war,

An iron factory in Pogradec supplies crucial building materials to Albania's construction industry.

Workers monitor a mixing machine at a cement factory. After World War II, the production of cement was one of the most important industries in Albania and in other Soviet-bloc countries. The rapid industrialization of these nations required the construction of new roads, buildings, and housing.

Courtesy of Illyria, The Albanian-American Newspaper, NY

the state built new industrial plants throughout the country. Following the Soviet model, Albania's leaders set production goals for the new factories, and all wages and prices came under strict central control.

Foreign aid and equipment, supplied by the Soviet Union and China, helped Albanian industries to grow dramatically during the 1950s and 1960s. New plants made paper, chemicals, glass, iron, and steel. Oil was refined and finished metals were exported. Small factories produced carpets, musical instruments, and other traditional Albanian crafts.

By the 1980s, industry made up two-thirds of Albania's total production of goods and services. But without new machinery and spare parts, factories soon became obsolete. Meanwhile, many Albanians took part in a private, underground market that supplied scarce consumer goods. This "black market" existed despite harsh penalties set down by Albania's leaders.

In the 1990s, the new government closed many inefficient industrial plants and ended price and wage controls. Albanian factories that are still operating make building materials—such as bricks, tiles, and cement—as well as furniture, textiles, shoes, and cigarettes. Food-processing firms prepare olive oil, sugar, and wine. Industrial products include chemicals and refined metals. A small output of television sets and radio receivers meets the growing demand for electronic goods in urban areas.

Agriculture and Forestry

Albania's Communist government undertook a massive reorganization of agriculture in the 1950s and 1960s. The regime forced rural laborers onto collectives, which were supposed to reach production quotas

53

In the early 1990s, Albanian farms—such as this one near Gjirokaster—were transferred from government ownership to private hands.

set by the government. Farmers had to sell their produce directly to the state at fixed prices. Albania also organized state farms, on which all managers and laborers became government employees.

New investment in modern farm machinery increased the output of collectives and state farms, and by the late 1970s Albania had achieved self-sufficiency in grain crops. But because the state set wages and prices, the collective workers had little incentive to further increase their harvests. Food production declined, and Albanians saw shortages of meat, vegetables, fruit, and dairy products.

Shepherds in northern Albania compare two small lambs from their herds.

In the 1980s, as the food supply dwindled, collective farmers joined townspeople in demanding economic reforms. After the fall of Communism, the new government set up village committees to return collective land to private farmers. By 1993 all Albanian farmland was again in private hands. Agriculture now makes up about 35 percent of the economy.

Seventy percent of Albania is mountainous, and little land is suitable for crop farming. The largest agricultural area lies in the western plains near the Adriatic Sea. The mild climate of this area helps farmers grow cotton, sugar beets, grapes, citrus fruits, rice, wheat, potatoes, and corn.

Other small plains and fertile valleys are scattered throughout the country. In the Korce Basin, for example, olive trees thrive. Farmers raise livestock—including sheep, poultry, goats, cattle, hogs, and horses—in highland pastures and coastal plains.

Albania's small forestry industry supplies wood mainly to the construction sector. Although forests cover about 43 percent of the land, overcutting has caused deforestation and erosion. In many areas, only shoots and shrubs survive. A small reforestation project is under way, but Albania continues to cut trees faster than they can be replaced.

Mining and Energy

With the assistance of the Soviet Union and China, the Albanian government invested in new mining equipment soon after World War II. When Albania became more isolated, the country found itself with no

These heavy logs will fuel the wood-burning furnaces that heat many Albanian homes and shops.

Miners examine train cars full of chromium ore, one of Albania's most valuable exports. The ore will be sold to foreign countries for refining into chrome, a material used in automobiles, appliances, and machinery.

Photo by Frank Jossi

Albania built large hydroelectric dams on the Drin River after World War II. The river's current was strong enough to generate surplus electricity that Albania sold to neighboring countries.

Photo by Albanian Telegraphic Agency

money to repair or replace old machinery. A lack of trained engineers also hurt the mining industry, slowing exploration for new mineral and oil deposits.

In the mid-1990s, minerals and finished metals again became important sources of export earnings. Miners at several sites extract chromite, a metallic ore used to produce chromium. Rising production has made Albania one of the world's largest suppliers of this metal, which is used in manufacturing. Albania also mines copper,

nickel, iron, and phosphate, a valuable fertilizer. Natural gas and coal are used to fuel factories and to heat homes. In addition, Italy and Saudi Arabia are working with Albania to explore offshore oil reserves along the Adriatic coast.

The Albanian government completed the electrification of the country in 1971. More than 80 percent of Albania's electricity comes from hydroelectric plants, two of which operate on the Drin River. Although Albanian power plants produce enough electricity for export, an inefficient transmission system still causes power outages in cities and rural areas.

Transportation and Tourism

Albania's only navigable river, the Buna, links Lake Shkoder with the Adriatic Sea. Most of the country's other waterways are used for hydroelectric production or for irrigation. Passenger ferries link the seaports of Durres and Vlore, and a small merchant fleet connects Albania's coastal cities with ports in Italy.

Albania's 8,100-mile road network consists of two-lane paved and unpaved roads. Because private cars were banned until 1990, most Albanians still use public transportation to get around the country.

Courtesy of Illyria, The Albanian-American Newspaper, NY

This new seaside resort near Sarande is ready for foreign visitors. Tourism along the undeveloped Adriatic coast may become an important part of the country's future economic growth.

Courtesy of Illyria, The Albanian-American Newspaper, NY

These residents of Berat are working to rebuild older homes that have fallen into disrepair.

Passengers crowd onto a bus in downtown Tirane. The rapid growth of the city is overloading the public transportation system.

A *tekke*, or Muslim monastery, sits at the end of a row of majestic cypress trees near Gjirokaster.

In the cities, buses, bicycles, and pedestrians greatly outnumber automobiles. The main airport at Tirane provides a link to several European nations, including Italy, Serbia, and Greece. The state-owned railway system covers 254 miles, with an international line running between Shkoder and Montenegro.

During the late 1980s, after the government of Ramiz Alia allowed tourists to enter Albania, about 20,000 foreign travelers visited each year. The new government sees tourism as a way of bringing in money that can be used for new investment. But the lack of good roads, hotels, and restaurants is slowing the growth of Albania's tourism industry. German, Italian, and Middle Eastern companies are planning to build new hotels and resorts that will meet the demands of vacationers.

Albania has many points of interest for foreign tourists. The southern Adriatic

Photo by Diane Katsiaficas

This banknote is worth 25 leks, the unit of Albanian currency. The note carries the Albanian coat of arms and a design celebrating agricultural workers.

coast offers quiet, uncrowded beaches from Vlore to Sarande. Durres boasts the largest ancient amphitheater in the Balkans, and important archaeological sites also exist at Apollonia and Butrint, in southern Albania. Well-preserved houses

Photo by Frank Jossi

This castle near Gjirokaster dates to the Ottoman occupation of Albania. Restored after World War II, the stronghold was used to imprison political opponents of the government.

Families wait for a ferry to dock in Durres. Ferries provide Albanians with the most reliable transportation across the Adriatic Sea to Italy.

Photo © Massimo Sciacca

that date back centuries line the winding, steep streets of Berat and Gjirokaster.

Adventurous tourists have also visited the rugged mountains of the north, where some of Albania's traditional clans have survived. The eastern lakes that Albania shares with Macedonia and Greece may soon be drawing visitors as well.

Foreign Trade

Since World War II, Albania's biggest trading partners have been its neighbors

On the walls of this shop in Durres, a sign marks the spot where police executed Albanian guerrillas during World War II. Many public monuments in Albania celebrate the struggle of Albania's wartime fighters, some of whom—including Enver Hoxha—became postwar leaders of the Communist government.

Photo © Massimo Sciacca

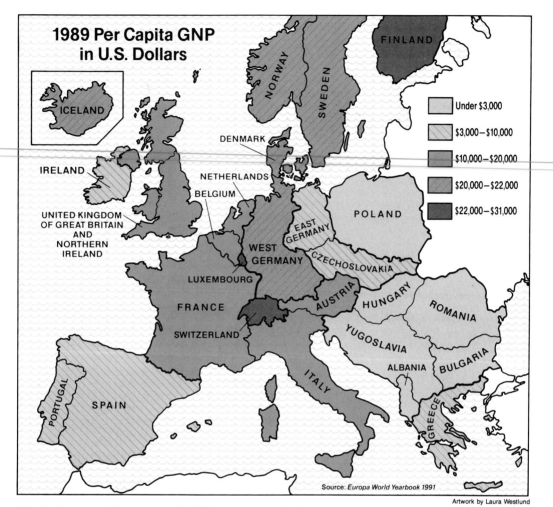

1989 Per Capita GNP in U.S. Dollars

Under $3,000

$3,000–$10,000

$10,000–$20,000

$20,000–$22,000

$22,000–$31,000

Source: *Europa World Yearbook 1991*

Artwork by Laura Westlund

This chart compares the average productivity per person—calculated by gross national product (GNP) per capita—for 26 European countries. The GNP is the value of all goods and services produced by a country in a year. With rapidly declining production and little foreign investment, Albania's 1989 GNP stood at $740 per capita, the lowest figure in Europe. Reforms put in place after the fall of the Communist regime caused some industries to decline and many factories to close. In the early 1990s, however, new investment—along with an open market for goods and services—helped the country's productivity improve.

on the Balkan Peninsula. But the civil war among the former Yugoslavian republics—and an international ban placed on trade with Serbia—greatly reduced Albania's commerce with this region in the early 1990s. Italy is now the country's chief trading partner. Italian companies are providing food, cars, machinery, and technicians to the growing Albanian market. Greece sells food products in Tirane and southern Albania.

Albania still has a trade deficit, meaning it buys more goods from abroad than it sells to foreign countries. Chromite, electricity, copper wire, tobacco, oil, and handicrafts are exported mostly to European countries, such as the Czech Republic, Italy, Bulgaria, and Germany. Many of the millions of Albanians who work abroad send money to their relatives in Albania, a practice that makes up a significant portion of the nation's total income. Albania

Photo © Massimo Sciacca

This woman has collected bread and vegetables during her morning shopping rounds. Often, however, Albanian shops have little fresh food available, and the lifting of price controls has made most goods and services more expensive.

imports machinery, fuels, chemicals, food, and consumer goods.

In 1990 the government began permitting foreign investors to form partnerships with Albanian firms. If the country's low production costs convince European, U.S., and Middle Eastern businesses to establish operations in Albania, the nation's exports could increase dramatically.

The Future

Compared to many other Balkan nations, Albania experienced a fairly smooth transition from Communism to democratic rule. Despite serious economic problems, the new government remains stable, and most Albanians are united in their support of economic reforms.

Yet war in the former Yugoslavia is threatening Albania. Kosovo's ethnic Albanians, who form the majority population in that region, are at odds with ethnic

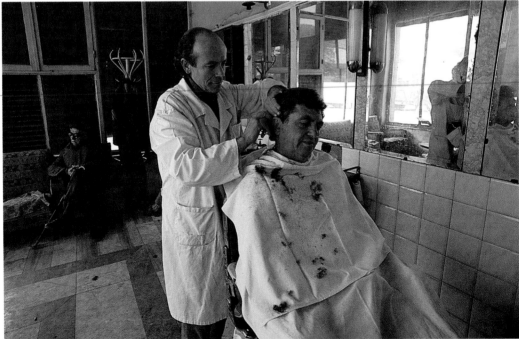

Photo © Massimo Sciacca

A barber plies his trade in Durres. Even barbers were once government employees, but now they run their shops as private businesses.

Boys play with dangerous toys in a rough Tirane neighborhood. One of the new quarters planned and built after World War II, this area of the city is officially known as Neighborhood #24.

Serbs and with the government of Serbia, which controls Kosovo as a semi-independent province. Thousands of Albanians have fled Kosovo and moved to Albania. As tension mounts, many experts worry that open conflict between Albania and Serbia may result.

Although the fear of spreading warfare in the Balkans is slowing foreign invest-ment in Albania, many international aid organizations have opened offices in Tirane. These groups can help the nation to rebuild roads, housing, agriculture, and schools. Tourism and the export of natural resources may also improve the economy. Many Albanians are hopeful for a better future, but the country faces the difficult job of building an entirely new economy.

Fishing boats cast their nets in the waters of Lake Prespa, where the borders of Macedonia, Albania, and Greece meet.

Index